WHOM THEY PIERCED

Whom They Pierced

BY

MERVYN STOCKWOOD
Vicar of St. Matthew, Moorfields, Bristol

WITH A FOREWORD
BY THE BISHOP OF LONDON

LONGMANS, GREEN AND CO.
LONDON ★ NEW YORK ★ TORONTO

LONGMANS, GREEN AND CO. LTD.
6 & 7 CLIFFORD STREET, LONDON, W.I
NICOL ROAD, BOMBAY I
17 CHITTARANJAN AVENUE, CALCUTTA 13
36A MOUNT ROAD, MADRAS 2

LONGMANS, GREEN AND CO. INC.
55 FIFTH AVENUE, NEW YORK 3

LONGMANS, GREEN AND CO.
215 VICTORIA STREET, TORONTO I

First published 1948

CODE NUMBER: 41214

PRINTED IN GREAT BRITAIN BY
THE BOWERING PRESS, PLYMOUTH

To the memory
of
ERIC LOVEDAY

FOREWORD

I FEEL sure that no one will read this devout and eloquent book without being deeply moved. It brings with it the atmosphere of the Three Hours' Service and will provide an excellent preparation for the most solemn season of the Christian year. And it will also lead us to examine our own lives and conduct with searching care to see how they may be made to conform more nearly to the pattern set by our Divine Lord. That after all should be the object of all our Lent reading.

✠ WM. LONDIN.

CONTENTS

INTRODUCTION

THIS book is based upon addresses given in London on two consecutive Good Fridays; in 1946 at Holy Trinity, Brompton, in 1947 at St. Martin's-in-the-Fields. They have, however, been re-written and many changes have been made.

The purpose of the book is devotional. I have not touched on the difficult doctrine of the Atonement, and I have avoided academic problems; instead I have tried to discuss some of the simpler and more practical implications of the Cross.

I am sure that Lent will be profitably spent if we can discover the difference which the fact of Calvary should make to our lives. We need to become so conscious of the death and resurrection of Jesus that all our decisions and actions are affected by them. We are often told that our country lacks spiritual power and vision. When we analyse such a statement it means that the men and women who live in these islands are unmindful of the presence of God as they set about their ordinary tasks. It is more than that—we must be certain that when we do think about God and try to obey His will, it is the God who is revealed in Jesus Christ.

I sometimes suggest to people that they should examine their lives and then ask themselves this question, "Suppose I had never heard of Jesus and there was no such thing as Christianity, would my life be different from what it is?" If we face the challenge honestly, we shall soon discover whether we have been influenced by the spirit of Calvary.

But the Cross is not only the criterion by which we judge ourselves and our practical effectiveness as Christians, it also quickens our spiritual perception in so far as it shows us the quality of God's love and the quality of man's sin. If we can consider these two things seriously we shall be led to a deeper understanding of the forgiveness and friendship of Jesus. Could anything be more important? We rightly have our schemes for furthering a religious revival and for making the Church more effective, but in the last resort our success or failure will depend upon the extent to which the individual Christian has found in Christ his living Lord and Saviour.

MERVYN STOCKWOOD

ST. MATTHEW, MOORFIELDS,
    BRISTOL.
Lent 1948.

Pilate brought Jesus out and seated him on the tribunal at a spot called the 'mosaic pavement'—the Hebrew name is Gabbatha (it was the day of the Preparation for the passover, about noon). "There is your king!" he said to the Jews. Then they yelled, "Off with him! Off with him! Crucify him!" "Crucify your king?" said Pilate. The high priest retorted, "We have no king but Caesar!" Then Pilate handed him over to them to be crucified. So they took Jesus, and he went away, carrying the cross by himself, to the spot called the 'place of the skull'—the Hebrew name is Golgotha; there they crucified him, along with two others, one on each side and Jesus in the middle. Pilate had written an inscription to be put on the cross; what he wrote was, Jesus the Nazarene, the King of the Jews. (St. John xix, 13-19.)

FIVE days ago it had seemed so full of hope. Jesus had been hailed as king. The people had cut down branches of trees to spread in the way. They had cried, "Hosanna!" Now all was lost. There is a crowd still, but not of friends. In their hands they carry not branches and palms, but swords and staves. They cry out not "Hosanna", but "Crucify". Why? I want to fasten your attention on this question. So much can depend upon your understanding of it, because, as we stand beneath the cross, we are not witnessing something which happened and finished hundreds of years ago; rather we are taking part in something which concerns us now. The issues which were fought out on Calvary are the issues which still divide civilisation. Just as on the first Good Friday men had to make up their minds whether they approved or disapproved of the Crucifixion, so to-day we have to come to a similar decision.

At a first glance, it would seem incredible that quite decent ordinary men and women could behave in such a way. Jesus had done them no harm, and yet they were clamouring for his blood. And the tragic fact which confronts the realist is that, although the mob may express its clamour differently, its demands are still the same. And by the mob I mean people like you and me. We may shudder at the thought of crucifixion, but because we cannot face the challenge which Jesus offers us, we try to be rid of him, usually by altering his Gospel to such an extent that we screen ourselves from its piercing truth with a deceptive shroud of pious jargon. I want to emphasise this, because Calvary is not necessarily the result of a wrong choice between an obvious good and an obvious evil, but between two types of good, the less apparent and the more apparent. Then there is no doubt that when three o'clock came on that Friday afternoon, there were many highly principled men in Jerusalem who conscientiously thought that the death of the rebel carpenter was in the best interests of religion. They felt that if he continued to proclaim his dangerous doctrines, the fabric of Judaism would be threatened. They were right. Their sin was in their inability to see that truth demanded that it should be so. Many of the worst features in the history of the Church and in the lives of Churchmen have been due to similar reasons. Conservative orthodoxy is too often afraid to pursue a path of spiritual and intellectual integrity because it suspects that the conclusions may be incompatible with its immediate interests.

Go back to the Palm Sunday procession and see if you can recognise yourself in it. The ex-carpenter of Nazareth is arriving at Jerusalem to make one final appeal. He comes as the Messiah, destined to set up God's Kingdom upon earth and to inaugurate a new ordering of society. Do not let us be in any doubt about that. It is no good trying to turn Jesus into a respectable clergyman leading his followers to the capital city on a Sunday School outing. In the eyes of many spectators he is an agitator, a revolutionary, a social menace, the sort of person, who, had he lived in our generation, might have been detained under the defence regulations for constituting a danger to national security. Worse still, he is summoning the people to co-operate with him.

That is where the trouble begins, because many who wave palms and shout "Hosanna", are not prepared to take risks or do anything which might jeopardise their futures. They are the people who shout much, but do little. They are ready to argue, to criticise, to sit on committees and to produce reports, but never to commit themselves. Consequently, when they see that Jesus is heading for crucifixion, they withdraw and leave him to his fate. He was never under any illusions about the difficulties which attend discipleship. He knew that sooner or later a man has to choose between loyalty to the Kingdom of God and loyalty to his own selfish interests. Some line of action is proposed, perhaps in personal affairs, or at work, or in the state, which is contrary to conscience, and a decision has to be made, and, as a result of that decision, the cause of the Kingdom is advanced or retarded.

There are others in that procession who are genuine well-wishers. They are attracted to Jesus. They believe in the new ordering of society which he has come to found, but, and how often there is a 'but', they are busy people and cannot devote much time to such things. They are incapable of realising

4

that a movement such as Jesus was launching can thrive, not upon occasional support, but upon persistent hard work.

So to-day we have our festivals and mass meetings, our sermons and conferences, but too often they are just flashes in the pan. Continuous hard grinding work and the readiness to fear nothing and to sacrifice everything are the only weapons capable of winning the war of God's Kingdom. We hear much of the failure of the Church. The parsons would be the first to admit their share of responsibility for it. But the laity must also realise that, without their unstinting efforts, there can be no success. Too often religious obligations are thought to be discharged by attendances at services and donations to church finances. These are important, but a great deal more is required of the man in the pew, if the country is to be won to Christ. He must strain every nerve to build up a Christian community in the parish where he lives. He must pull his weight in bringing influence to bear upon the bodies which frame our national and social life. It is, for instance, useless to complain of the indifference towards religion unless we are prepared to find Christians, if need be ourselves, to serve on these bodies. If Churchmen are content to regard golf, tennis or gardening as alternatives to public service, then it is inevitable that public life will be directed by the non-Christians who care sufficiently for their particular beliefs to find the necessary time.

Others take their place in the Palm Sunday crowd because they want Jesus to do something for them. The fact that he is out to change the world and to liberate mankind does not concern them; all they care about is his ability to satisfy their immediate needs. A friend is in trouble, a relative is sick, somebody has died. If it can be brought to the notice of Jesus, he will put things right.

So to-day there are people who try to use religion and to manipulate the Church for their own ends. The fact that the primary reason for the Church's existence is to further the Kingdom of God does not impress them; they are quite satisfied with the world as it is, and they are much too timid and selfish to embark upon the adventure of changing it. But if things go wrong, they sincerely expect Christianity to help them. I remember a discussion in a military hospital shortly before VE-Day in which several soldiers were pouring scorn upon religion. They were silenced when a young private said, "You can talk like that now, but you were glad enough to get down on your knees and pray to God on the Normandy beaches on D-Day". Again, at the beginning of the war, I remember a Cabinet Minister, who prior to 1939 had jeered at the Church, changing his attitude completely, because he thought that, as the country was involved in war, the Church would now be useful for public morale. The soldiers and the Cabinet Minister are not isolated instances. Any parish priest could quote examples of people who come to him in the hope of getting something for nothing out of the Church. They expect to buy cheaply without paying the spiritual and moral prices of discipleship. Sometimes their attitude is conspicuously blameworthy, sometimes it is due to sheer blindness. They are as ignorant of the meaning of Christianity as were some of those who waved palms and shouted "Hosanna" on the first Palm Sunday. And it is worth remembering that in their case blindness was partly due to a Jewish Church which had failed to open their eyes. Moreover it is significant that Christ's first act upon reaching the Holy City was to challenge the whole ecclesiastical system by purging the temple courts. Here, too, we have something to learn to-day.

We cannot leave the procession without taking a look at the ass—and for the thoughts about him I am indebted to the late vicar of All Saints', Margaret Street, Dom Bernard Clements, who once preached a striking sermon on the subject at Cambridge when I was an undergraduate. You may read it for yourselves in his book of Holy Week meditations, *The Royal Banners*. The ass waves no palms, shouts no Hosannas;

yet he is nearer than anyone to Jesus and is doing most for him. It is not an enviable position. The hot clothes over his head, the branches of trees under his stumbling feet, the noise of the yelling mob, all combine to make his task more difficult than usual. Yet tired, hot and thirsty though he is, he carries the master to his destination. True religion is like that. We have wonderful dreams of Christianity's future; we attend stirring rallies at the Albert Hall; we read moving reports on the conversion of England; but, when we get home, there is still the washing-up to be done, still the awkward relative with whom to share the kitchen, still that dreary routine job in the factory and office. But it is these small every-day events which provide us with our opportunities. Perhaps when he thinks we are ready, Christ will ask us to carry him on a more thrilling journey; but he will never do this until he has proved us in the less interesting thoroughfares. Archbishop Temple was once approached by an Oxford undergraduate who said that he had been so moved by his sermon that he wanted to give up everything for Christ and his Church. "Good," said the Archbishop. "Now go back to your college and concentrate upon getting first-class honours in your degree." That is a parable which we can all take to heart. Most of us have got to stay where we are, and we must serve the master in our present circumstances. Let us make the most of the opportunities, no matter how unspectacular they may be. If we are to get the most from these meditations on the Cross, it means that when we have finished, we must be a little more like the ass which carried Jesus than we are now.

Christ goes forward to his Kingdom. We are carrying him, and the road takes us to the hill of Calvary. And it is at Calvary that we make our halt. Immediately we are confronted by a terrible fact—a peasant labourer, stripped of his possessions, deserted by his friends is fast dying on a common gallows. And this terrible fact is demanding of us the readiness to put ourselves completely at his disposal.

> In thy most bitter passion
> My heart to share doth cry.
> With thee for my salvation
> Upon the cross to die.
> Ah, keep my heart thus moved
> To stand thy cross beneath,
> To mourn thee, well-beloved,
> Yet thank thee for thy death. Amen.

O Christ, the Master Carpenter, who at the last through wood and nails, purchased man's whole salvation, wield well thy tools in the workshop of this world, so that we, who come rough-hewn to thy bench, may here be fashioned to a truer beauty by thine hand. Amen.

Almighty God, we beseech thee graciously to behold this thy family, for which our Lord Jesus Christ was contented to be betrayed, and given up into the hands of wicked men, and to suffer death upon the Cross, who now liveth and reigneth with thee and the Holy Ghost, ever one God, world without end. Amen.

II

Jesus said, "Father, forgive them, they do not know what they are doing." (St. Luke xxiii,34.)

THUS Our Lord obeys his own command, "Love your enemies, do good to those who hate you: bless those who curse you, pray for those who abuse you." It is terrible to think of the savagery with which the nails were driven into the hands and feet of Jesus; yet it is even more stirring to think of the heart which never ceased to love the perpetrators of such a crime. That is something we find so hard to imitate. When we talk about forgiving others, it usually means the attempt to ignore an unpleasant episode about which we harbour a legion of black and revengeful thoughts. Sometimes we say, "I've forgiven him, but I shall never be able to forget". And, in our mind's eye, we live through the scene again, considering the cruel things we might have said and thinking of the remarks we shall make when next we see him, and the criticisms we shall offer to our friends to arouse their pity on our behalf.

If forgiveness is to be real, it means that our attitude towards those who have offended us must be similar to that of Jesus towards the soldiers who crucified him. So far as we are concerned there must be no barriers. Instead we must see to it that, whenever the other person wants to put things right, we shall go more than half-way to meet him, even if in so doing our pride is severely humbled. That is the lesson we learn from the parable of the prodigal son. In the heart of the father, unlike that of the self-righteous son, there is no resentment, no self-pity, no desire for revenge, but simply a longing to restore the child into the warmth and love of the family circle. He is concerned not with the injury which he has sustained, but with the violation which the son has done to his own personality.

I once knew a mother who, for her son's education, sacrificed everything, necessities as well as comforts. Not only was he unappreciative, but the day came when, after some years in a bank, he was convicted of fraud and sent to prison. Several months later he was let out. He was welcomed home and no mention was made of his misfortune. But the son was still untouched, and it was not long before he was back in prison for a similar offence. When the sentence was served, that brave and noble woman went to the prison gates to meet him and then, when they got home, showed him, not to his own room, but to the guest room, the place of special honour. That broke him. He was ready for criticism, ready for punishment, ready to be disinherited, ready to face it all and to go on rebelling. The thing for which he was not ready was that patient suffering love which never took offence, never failed to forgive, never ceased being eager to re-establish, without any conditions, a broken family relationship.

It is forgiveness of this quality which characterises the life of Jesus, not only on Good Friday, but always. Do you remember how, early on Good Friday, Peter denied his Master? Three times he cursed violently, not because he was ashamed of himself, but because his pride was hurt. A few hours before he had made an extravagant boast about his loyalty, saying he was prepared to suffer a martyr's death. It had been big talk which had gone down well. Now he was making a pitiful fool of himself in public, and he disliked the humiliation of it. And then something happened. He forgot his pride and went out into the night and poured out his heart in tears. The Lord had turned and looked upon Peter; and Peter saw in those loving eyes the agony of a passionate forgiveness which offered him unconditional friendship.

Earlier in his ministry Jesus showed this same forgiveness to Zacchaeus, a man who had done much harm to his fellow men by his anti-social behaviour. Most people would have ignored him, but not so Our Lord. He cared for him. He was concerned not with the criticisms of the past, but with the possibilities of the future. He certainly did not condone his dealings with the poor and his methods of exploitation, but he realised that men like Zacchaeus will come to themselves, not by moral condemnations, but by large-hearted kindliness. And the greatness of Jesus is to be seen in his ability to put the personality of the offender before all other considerations. He knew that when a man did wrong, the chief sufferer was the man himself, in so far as evil violates the character of the perpetrator.

And so as we stand beneath the Cross our Lord challenges us. What is the quality of our forgiveness? When a barrier separates us from somebody else, do we care so much for the person on the other side of the barrier that we do our best to pull it down, or do we behave as though our pride were the most important factor in the situation, claiming that we need make no move until we have received satisfaction in the form of an apology?

During the war when preaching one Good Friday on this first word from the Cross, I said we must apply Christ's standards of forgiveness to our enemies and that in the silence which followed the address I intended to pray for the German people. Six of the congregation immediately left the church in protest. They failed to realise that the characteristic of

Christian forgiveness is the patient desire that the offender shall be restored to fellowship. They had not grasped that Christians are expected to forgive all men and not just those they happen to like. But what was worse, they had not learnt that it is not our prerogative to decide who may or may not be forgiven. No matter how seriously other people may sin, most of us have enough sins of our own to prevent us from setting ourselves up as judges. In this particular instance only the morally blind would attribute the sole responsibility for the war to the Germans. Most of us remember too well the activities of some of our countrymen who aided Hitler and supplied his gangsters with money and armaments. Let Englishmen be humble before God about their own national crimes before they start to judge others.

Then I want you to be practical in your private relationships. Think of the people you dislike because they have injured you. Perhaps it is a relation, somebody at the office, a neighbour in the street, or perhaps it is your husband. Are you going to allow these barriers which divide you to remain, or will you pocket your pride and for Christ's sake break them down? You may well be snubbed and nothing may come of your efforts, but it is your duty to try.

And what of the quality of forgiveness in our church life? For the man who has sinned and is eager to make a fresh start nothing is more helpful than a church which permeates through its fellowship the spirit of forgiving love and healing friendship. On the other hand for such a man there is nothing more soul-destroying than a church which, lacking this real fellowship, is quick to criticise and slow to show mercy. Perhaps this is a reason why some demobilised soldiers have left their churches with a heavy heart. They tried to make a fresh start, but the older people who were firmly fixed in a rut gave them not encouragement, but criticism. How sadly we ignore our Lord's commands. On Easter Day he told his followers that they were to liberate men from their sins, and this instruction is repeated in the Anglican service of Ordination. This may involve a formal absolution in an ecclesiastical context, but it will achieve little unless the priest who pronounces the absolution and the people associated with him adopt a constructive attitude towards the penitent.

Many years ago when I was looking after a small mission, a young man in my congregation was involved in a serious scandal. What concerned me was not the criticism which outsiders might level at the church, but the fear that my own people might adopt an attitude which would make it difficult for him to start afresh. So, with his permission, I told the congregation of his mistake and that he had received from me, in the name of the whole Church, the assurance of Christ's forgiveness. "It is now up to you", I added, "to make that forgiveness a reality." They saw what I meant. They abstained from criticism and although they were very poor, they gave him financial help. What was more important they made him feel that he was still a valued member of the family circle.

There is one other lesson we can learn as we listen to the first word from the Cross; it is this. Our readiness to forgive others will depend upon our experience of having been forgiven. The man who has first-hand knowledge of the forgiving love of Christ is the man who is most likely to extend that love to others.

I think we miss this note of repentance in some of our preaching to-day, with the result that we have underestimated the gravity of sin. Our grandfathers may have obeyed God for fear of the consequences, and, although the motive is scarcely satisfactory, there is something to be said for it. It did, at least, encourage a person to put God's will before self-will, because it was certain that one day there would be a reckoning before the judgment seat. It may be necessary for us to explain these ideas differently, but we must be careful not to explain them away. God's law must be obeyed. If we ignore it, we do so at our peril. Moreover sin separates a soul from God and there can be no happiness and peace so long as these dividing barriers remain.

At the same time if a man will humbly acknowledge his failures, if he will admit that the evil in him cuts him off from the true source of his being, he will experience the joys of forgiveness and liberation. But he must be strictly honest with himself when taking this step. It is possible to say the general confession in church without facing the deep inner conflicts in our lives which are at the root of our troubles. We need not belong to the Oxford Group to realise that there can be no real peace of soul until Sin has been fairly and squarely faced and confessed. That is why there is much to be said for availing ourselves of sacramental absolution. The Church of England is opposed to compulsory confession to a priest, but it makes provision for it and, in some circumstances, encourages it. Psychological research in recent years suggests that many casualties would have been avoided if more use had been made of it. I am not suggesting that the primary purpose of sacramental confession is to provide the patient with a sense of release; on the contrary it is to give the penitent the assurance of Christ's forgiving love, but in doing this it will at the same time help him to achieve integration of personality.

As we listen to this first word from the Cross, let us be challenged by it. Are we facing our sins and the forgiveness which Christ offers? Or are we holding something back, some secret sin which has us in its grip, some wrong practice which we are unwilling to sacrifice, some bad relationship which is spoiling our life at home or at work? If so, we shall carry with us a sense of defeat and guilt which will inevitably cripple our spirits.

But be certain of this, for the heart which is truly penitent, there is a promise of forgiveness and victory which has only to be put to the test to be found true. No matter how far we may have fallen, there is a way back. We may have disgraced our birthright, but he is waiting to welcome us as sons. That is what Christ now offers us from his Cross. It is up to us to throw ourselves upon his mercy and to accept his gift humbly.

O Holy Spirit, renew us day by day and fashion us after the image of God; let all bitterness be put away from us, all evil speaking and all unkind thoughts. May we be kind one to another, forgiving one another even as we, through the Cross, are forgiven. Amen.

O Christ, the true vine and the source of life, ever giving thyself that the world may live: who also has taught us that those who would follow thee must be ready to lose their lives for thy sake; grant us so to receive within our souls the power of thine eternal sacrifice, that in sharing thy cup we may share thy glory, and at the last be made perfect in thy love. Amen.

Grant, we beseech thee, merciful Lord, to thy faithful people, pardon and peace, that they may be cleansed from all their sins, and serve thee with a quiet mind; through Jesus Christ our Lord. Amen.

III

*The people stood and stared, while the rulers sneered
at him, saying, "He saved others, let him save himself,
if he is the Christ of God, the Chosen One!" The
soldiers made fun of him too by coming up and handing
him vinegar, saying, "If you are the King of the Jews,
save yourself." (For there was an inscription over him
in Greek and Latin and Hebrew characters,* THIS IS
THE KING OF THE JEWS.) *One of the criminals who
had been hanged also abused him, saying, "Are you not
the Christ? Save yourself and us as well." But the
other checked him, saying, "Have you no fear even of
God? You are suffering the same punishment as he.
And we suffer justly; we are getting what we deserve for
our deeds. But he has done no harm." And he added,
"Jesus, do not forget me when you come to reign." "I
tell you truly," said Jesus, "you will be in paradise
with me this very day."* (St. Luke xxiii, 35-45.)

ALTHOUGH the public memory is short-lived, I doubt
whether this generation will forget the last days of
the Nazi regime in the spring of 1945. If the reports
are true, Hitler was in his shelter in Berlin preparing
for suicide. A defeated man, pursued by his own

crimes and wickedness, he was left with only one means of escape, death. Those associated with him knew that they too were involved in a disaster which was beyond redemption. The dreams had turned into nightmares. The conquests, the rallies, the bravado, the struttings, were being overtaken by a terrible nemesis—complete failure and destruction.

How different, we think, were the last hours of Jesus. But would we have thought so if we had been on Calvary when it all happened? Is it not more likely that we should have shared the general opinion, which was that a young and misguided revolutionary was receiving his reward as a failure?

For three years the ex-carpenter had tramped the country asserting that he had been sent by God to inaugurate a new ordering of society, and now he was confronted by disaster—disaster characterised by a cross for a throne and thorns for a crown. What is remarkable are not the sneers of the crowd expressed so contemptuously in the remark, "He saved others, let him save himself, if he is the Christ of God", but the act of faith on the part of the criminal dying along-side him. "Jesus, do not forget me when you come to reign." Those of you who have stood at the death beds of people in great agony would readily excuse the dying for not showing much interest in the world in which they live, or in the leader of some newfangled revolution. And yet this poor wretched thief in his extremity could apparently see what others could not, that Jesus is King, and that his Kingdom is a reality. We can imagine how much this must have meant to Our Lord. As the shadows of death speedily gathered round him, somebody had at last made the discovery which he himself had made in the solitude of the wilderness three years before.

When Jesus was thirty he knew that his Father had singled him out for some particular work concerned with the inauguration of the Kingdom of God upon earth. So he downed tools and joined his fellow countrymen, in the Jordan valley, who were awaiting the Messiah. It is possible that when John the Baptist hailed him as the Messiah, he was taken by surprise. In any case it was an unenviable position. The Messiah was, in popular judgment, to usher in a golden age of peace and prosperity, a task as difficult to accomplish then as it is to-day. Imagine yourself in his position. Upon your actions depends the destiny of the world. To you is entrusted the task of accomplishing the divine will and of redeeming mankind. Faced with such a responsibility Jesus went into the desert to think things over and to plan a campaign.

Now, if you want to build a new world, you must have the backing of a large section of the people; and you will only get this backing if they are convinced of the worthwhileness of your programme. Jesus knew that, and it was about the question of a programme that he had to wage such a fierce struggle. Like other leaders he knew that the easiest way to obtain popular support was to appeal to men's stomachs. In this case there was an additional reason. Palestine was an occupied country, and the Jews longed to be rid of the invaders and to turn their distressed land into an oasis of peace and plenty. Jesus never despised men's economic needs. It is a travesty of the Gospel to pretend that it is an other-worldly religion, not concerned with material, social and political conditions. Jesus was always the champion of the poor, the distressed, the exploited and the under-dog. And we must never forget that, no matter how much we may dislike the fact and try to gloss it over, the immediate cause of the crucifixion was a political accusation. But that was not all. He was not just a social reformer. He believed that men should have bread, but that their true natures could not be satisfied on the material level alone. He knew that a new world, such as he wanted, could not be built by social legislation only. Important though it certainly is to plan economic resources in such a way that all men may have their reasonable needs met, yet man is something more than a creature of economics. Man's main problem is himself, and Jesus

24

knew that there was little hope for the world until man had faced the challenge of the living God in his life. By all means have enlightened political and economic programmes, but never lose sight of the main truth that more important than any programme is the conversion of men's souls. The tragedy of the Church is that these two approaches have been set the one against the other. The first is regarded as political, the second as spiritual. In fact both must go together, for either by itself inevitably leads to a travesty of the Gospel.

You will see the same truth revealed in the other temptations. They encourage Jesus to build his new world with false weapons, and he rejects them because he knows that the result will be a sham. Although men will be stirred by false faiths and programmes of expediency, yet they will be stirred for the wrong reasons; and although they may build a new world, it will not be a world in which God reigns as King. Jesus could have thrown himself from the temple and he might have been unscathed, but it is unlikely that the effects would have been morally desirable. Crowds will flock to a wonder-worker for reasons of idle curiosity, but miracles can increase rather than diminish spiritual blindness. I remember how in the early days of ministry I was asked to administer spiritual healing to a man who was dangerously ill.

He had a remarkable physical recovery, but it did nothing to hasten his conversion. On the contrary, he regarded me as a magician whose charms were more successful and less expensive than the doctor's. During the war this attitude could be detected in national days of prayer. Dunkirk may have been the consequence of our intercessions and, at the time, it caused considerable interest; but there is little to suggest that it helped towards a large-scale revival of religion or of spiritual awareness.

Similarly a new world based upon power politics with no regard to moral values can provide superficial attractions, but sooner or later disillusion follows. Most revolutions are engineered by enthusiasts who sincerely desire better conditions. But too often they are corrupted by power, because they decide that their determination to further their aims by any and every means justifies the violation of the sacredness of human personality. I am not suggesting that the issue is always obvious, especially as the opportunities for self-deception are enormous. The political agitator, whose philosophy is defective, tricks himself into believing that 'the masses' are yearning for him to assume power, and to confer upon them the benefits of his creed. In fact 'the masses' probably want nothing of the sort. So the agitator, now secure in a government position, uses force to give them what he thinks they ought to have. It is indeed a cruel dilemma, and one which confronts every politician from brightest blue to darkest red.

"You must worship the Lord your God, and serve him alone." There is no short cut to the Kingdom of Heaven; no method but this. So Jesus decides to use it. It may be political suicide, but he is determined to confront men one by one with the challenge of the living God. He is going to appeal not only to their economic needs, but to their reasons and their spiritual perception. God has a plan for the world. He has a plan for men. And this plan can only succeed when man becomes aware of his true destiny. Created in the image of God, he is meant for fellowship with God. This means that by constant communion with the Source of his being, he must strive in all things to obey His will.

This is a lesson which we urgently need to re-learn to-day. While we must strive to alter the world for the better—in fact, Christians should be pioneers in social and political movements—yet we shall fail in our task unless God is the beginning and end of our labours and the inspiration of our every action. This does not mean that we should cut ourselves off from our fellows on the ground that they are actuated by the wrong motives: still less does it imply that we should start some fresh Christian party to set itself up in judgment over other organisations. Rather we must take our places in the existing institutions, trying by our example and witness to supply the leaven. It is useless to imagine that we must wait for the ideal situation to emerge before we take action. On the contrary we must deal with men as they are and place ourselves alongside them, realising that the God who used ordinary flesh and blood to reveal himself at Bethlehem can take our present circumstances and use them for the redemption of the world.

Something of this, the thief grasped in the last minutes of his agony. We do not know for what reasons he had become a criminal, but in all probability he thought that the most certain way to obtain happiness was to pursue his selfish interests at the expense of the community. Now as he dies alongside Jesus he sees the futility of it all. He knows that the only kingdom which his methods can build is the kingdom of hell, whereas Jesus, because of his complete obedience to God, has shown where the secret of the new and better world is to be found. And, one minute to midnight though it is, he makes a simple act of faith in which he expresses his longing to be identified with his newly found Master. "Jesus, do not forget me when you come to reign."

What more can I say? Just this. We may not be guilty of crimes which lead to the gallows, but some of us are just as mistaken as the thief. And some of us are as lonely. We know that when the camouflage is stripped from us, we stand revealed as men with wrong values and an unworthy goal. We may talk about building a better world, but there is little that we can do about it, as our souls are paralysed.

If you are like that, turn to the Cross and look at Truth. "Jesus, do not forget me when you come to reign." You will not ask in vain. "I tell you truly, you will be in paradise with me this very day."

O Father of all men, who hast promised that the kingdoms of this world shall become the kingdom of thy Son: purge the nations of error and corruption; incline the hearts of all rulers and peoples to the Lord of Lords and King of Glory; scatter every excuse of frailty and unworthiness; consecrate us with a passion for thy rulership; and give us the grace and power to further thy purpose in the world for Christ's sake. Amen.

O king of men and master of our lives, entering into glory by thy Cross, to whom all authority is given both in heaven and upon earth: come, Christ, enter into thy kingdom; subdue the world by the power of thy love, and be known and adored to all the ends of the earth. Amen.

Almighty and most merciful God, of whose only gift

it cometh that thy faithful people do unto thee true and laudable service; grant, we beseech thee, that we may so faithfully serve thee in this life that we fail not finally to attain thy heavenly promises; through the merits of Jesus Christ our Lord. Amen.

IV

Now beside the cross of Jesus stood his mother and his mother's sister, Mary the wife of Clopas, and Mary of Magdala. So when Jesus saw his mother and his favourite disciple standing near, he said to his mother, "Woman, there is your son!" Then he said to the disciple, "And there is your mother!" And from that hour the disciple took her to his home. (St. John xix, 25-27.)

THIS is, I suppose, the most humanly moving word from the Cross, for who cannot feel the suffering which was his as he looked down upon the shattering grief of his mother? There must always be a poignancy, so stirring as to defeat description, in the sight of a mother desperately striving to hold back the fast-ebbing life of the son she loves. Now, indeed, was the prophecy of old Simeon fulfilled, "And your own soul will be pierced by a sword". To-day it had pierced to the hilt. Worse still, Jesus had to witness it all before his dying eyes. What memories must have crowded in upon his mind, memories of a happy childhood and a perfect home life, memories of the unfailing love of a mother who, although she may not always have understood, had never ceased to care.

And now it seemed that he had failed her. In addition to the shame of crucifixion and the tragedy of bereavement, there was the realisation that her hopes and dreams were apparently ruined. Time was running out. There was so little that he could do. He commended her to the care of his dearest friend.

Yet it is not the note of pathos that I would sound; rather I would draw your attention to the challenge which this third word from the Cross affords us.

First, as we think of the relationship which existed between this mother and son, we are driven to use it as the standard by which to judge the relationships within our own family circle. Too often it is the one place where we fail so badly. We find each other difficult. We regard our relations as peculiar and hard to understand. We allow minor irritations to become the cause of bitter quarrels. We expect the family circle to centre around our selfish inclinations and we resent interruptions from others. The result is that we become estranged and allow barriers to spring up. The atmosphere is vitiated and love begins to die.

There were problems in the home at Nazareth. Things were not always easy. When Jesus began to get into trouble with the authorities, Mary, like all mothers, began to interfere and, in the hope of saving her son from possible danger, advocated a policy of caution. Again, there were occasions when she simply did not understand him, and was perplexed beyond measure by the things he said and did. And sometimes there was a severity in his attitude, almost amounting to ruthlessness, which must have caused many a heart-ache. But in spite of it all, there was a spirit of give and take, of love and comradeship, which held good even in the blackest hours.

So then, what of our family relationships? Dare we let our contemplation of the Cross pass without a real attempt to put things right, by breaking down those barriers of estrangement which have sprung up between husband and wife, parents and children, and which are spoiling the atmosphere of our homes? Remember, there is no greater witness to the Christian Faith than a home which radiates the spirit which permeated the home at Nazareth, and there is nothing more damaging than a home which, while professing to be Christian, is conspicuous for its disunity and selfishness.

Selfishness is the cause of most domestic troubles. Like other parsons I have been involved in many disputes arising from the breakdown of family life during the war, and in nearly every case the crash could have been avoided if the parties concerned had been a little less selfish. Temptations inevitably follow separation and personal discipline is necessary if they are to be surmounted. Alas, such discipline is all too rare.

Now that the war is over, our difficulties are not at an end. It is not easy to settle down to the routine of home life after the comparatively free and easy atmosphere of the Forces. Such readjustment demands effort. I can think of a girl who married in 1941 a soldier who was demobilised five years later. She was really fond of him, but his complete lack of consideration for her eventually killed her love. He went to the pictures three times a week and to a football match on Saturdays. He never asked his wife to accompany him, but left her at home, night after night, to look after the baby. The girl said to me, "I dread it when the hands of the clock point to five o'clock because it means that Jack is on his way back. He sits down at the table, hardly speaks a word unless it's a grumble, and then he goes off for the evening. It used to be so different before we were married." It's easy for Jack to blame the war, but it is not an adequate excuse. His root trouble is selfishness and he is not prepared to master it.

At this point may I address a word to those growing up? Quite often parents in my parish will complain about the behaviour of their children and they ask me to speak to them. When an appropriate moment comes I try to broach the subject tactfully, and in most cases the boy or girl will reply, "I know what you mean, Vicar, but you don't understand my mother. She's becoming impossible. Her ideas are so old fashioned and she treats me as though I were still a child. I'm just not going to put up with it any more. I mean to be my own master." Yes, it is true that mothers are inclined to keep their children to their apron strings—just as you will, when you are a parent, because all the things you have said will be repeated about you by your sons and daughters—but meanwhile remember that, although it is right for you to want a reasonable amount of independence, you have certain obligations to your home. Do not treat it like a hotel, a place where you just eat and sleep. Remember, too, that no matter how awkward your mother and father may be, their hopes, their joys and their love are centred in you. Relationships between parents and children need delicate handling. We have dispensed with the heavy Victorian father, but I am not sure we have discovered a satisfactory substitute. At the risk of being condemned as a reactionary by the psychologists, I dare to confess that I am a firm believer in discipline. Liberty is a worthy ideal, but it needs to be distinguished from laxity and irresponsibility. While I have a great admiration for the younger generation and feel that in many ways it is more intelligent and enlightened than its pre-decessors, yet I think it would lose nothing if it had a greater awareness of its obligations and was a little readier to obey rules.

Secondly, this word from the Cross emphasises the importance of using common sense. Although Jesus was in his last agony, he realised that it was his duty as a son to make provision for his widowed mother, so he committed her to the keeping of John. It may seem a small point, but it is these little things in life which make so much difference. A wise husbanding of resources, a careful planning of expenditure, details of time, punctuality and tidiness are all matters of common sense, but common sense is a virtue which should characterise every Christian home. Moreover, if we have property, it is our duty to provide for its disposal in the event of our death. How often people are put to unnecessary trouble and expense because of the absence of a will. Perhaps this may seem out of place in our meditation on the last hours of Christ's life, but I believe the making of a will to be a practical implication of his third word.

Thirdly, it is a challenge to our courtesy. In spite of the agonising pain, Jesus thinks of his mother and his dearest friend. In desperate need himself, he puts their needs before his own. The French have a beautiful phrase for courtesy, *la politesse du coeur*. It is difficult to give a satisfactory translation in English —good manners, yes; but it is more than that. It suggests good manners not learnt from a book of rules, but flowing from a gracious and courteous heart and shown in the tone of voice, the ability to hold the tongue at the right moment, the understanding smile, the readiness to be polite and gentle in little things.

A young R.A.F. pilot had crashed and was severely burnt. His mother had motored miles to the hospital to share the last sacrament with him. The service finished, the boy smiled and then, as he closed his eyes to die, he whispered to the priest, "Padre, take mother out; it will be easier for her if she has not to watch me die."

La politesse du coeur. We do not need to wait for a cross or a death-bed before we can show the beauty of courtesy. Each day there are opportunities to prove by look, by smile, by tone of voice, by action, whether or not we share the secret of the politeness of the heart.

And how important is the quality of courtesy in our homes, shown in the way we address each other; in the deference of the men towards the women folk; in the treating of the domestic staff as members of the family circle with rights equal to our own; in the way we speak when we feel tired and out of sorts; in the realisation that at all times we must suppress signs of irritation, anger, or selfish and depressing moods. Such is courtesy, that quality of unfailing consideration which we see in this third word from the Cross.

Fourthly, it is a challenge to our attitude towards the place of women in society. It is impossible to assess the influence of Mary in the life of Jesus, but it is evident that the environment in which he was brought up played a considerable part in determining his character. It was Mary who first spoke to him of his Father, who made him familiar with the aspirations of the Jewish nation, who taught him the Scriptures; and it was Mary who, by her own example, showed him the possibilities which result from a heart fully surrendered to God.

It is a pity that in the effort to discard the false doctrines which surrounded the Virgin in the Middle Ages, the English people, at the Reformation, went to the other extreme, with the result that there is now little reverence for the mother of Jesus. It is time that we pursued a more moderate policy by restoring her to her proper place. If we do that we may give a fresh dignity to family life in general and to motherhood in particular. No nation can flourish unless it is built upon the sanctity of the home, and there is more than enough evidence to suggest that in this respect England is sadly deficient. Divorce, the refusal to have children and the disruption of family ties are hastening the disintegration of society, and it is time that men who care for the future of our country, whether Christian or not, should see the red light before it is too late and we go the way of the Roman empire.

When Jesus entrusted Mary to John, he was symbolically entrusting the institution of motherhood and the family to his followers. For Christians to-day this has many implications. They include such straightforward material benefits as family allowances, clinics, improved housing conditions, sex education and sufficient leisure. But more important than any material benefit is an attitude towards motherhood based upon the conviction that it is of divine ordinance. The Church has many battles to win, but the most decisive of all is the battle for the Christian home. It may be difficult for us to see what we can do to solve the big problems which face our civilisation, but there is one thing which is in the grasp of all of us—the determination to model our family life upon the home at Nazareth. If we can produce a noble generation of mothers, fathers and children, we shall do more than a little to bring light to the dark places of the world and to lay the foundations of a healthier ordering of society.

O Lord Jesus Christ, who, on the Cross, didst remember thy mother and thy friend, make our homes to be homes of courtesy and gentle understanding. Spread thy grace over every relationship of human life, so that all our earthly love may be gathered up into the love of God and thy kingdom made manifest to men in the homes of thy people. Amen.

O God, who art present in every place and from whose love no space or distance can separate us, grant us to know that those who are absent from one another are still present with thee: and though separated may we realise our fellowship with one another in our common service of thee; through Jesus Christ our Lord. Amen.

Almighty God, our heavenly father, whose blessed Son did share at Nazareth the life of an earthy home: Bless, we beseech thee, the homes of our children, and grant wisdom and understanding to all who have the care of them. Amen.

V

*Now from twelve o'clock to three o'clock darkness
covered all the land, and about three o'clock Jesus gave
a loud cry,*" Eli, eli, lema sabachthani" (*that is, My
God, my God, why forsake me?*). *On hearing this,
some of the bystanders said, "He is calling for Elijah".
One of them ran off at once and took a sponge, which he
soaked in vinegar and put on the end of a stick, to give
him a drink. But the others said, "Stop, let us see if
Elijah does come to save him!" (Seizing a lance, another
pricked his side, and out came water and blood.)*
(St. Matthew XXVII, 45-49.)

IT is easy to appreciate the human appeal of this
fourth word from the Cross. A young man, his life
hardly begun, is fast dying with a sense of hopeless
failure. Mocked by his enemies, betrayed and deserted by his friends, he is left alone—alone in a
darkness as intense as the sense of frustration which
bears in upon his soul.

Yet there is something more terrible about this
utterance than its aspect of human suffering. The cry
of Jesus is no cry of pity for himself, but the expres-
sion of a ghastly fear that God's purpose for the
restoration of the world has been thwarted. As he

hangs there it is as a king who has lost his Kingdom, as the Saviour of a world which has rejected the salvation which he has come to offer. For as the darkness descended upon the Cross Jesus did not know what we, living nineteen hundred years later, know. To suppose that he could at that particular moment foresee the triumph of his passion with all its victorious implications, is to minimise the doctrine of the Incarnation with its insistence upon the genuineness of Christ's manhood.

So as you see him hanging in the shadows and hear that bitter, piercing cry of distress, realise that Jesus is experiencing that agony of soul which comes to a man who believes that his efforts to achieve the things which are right and good have ended in catastrophe. Three years before the heavens had opened before him and he had offered himself to the Father for the task of building his kingdom upon earth. Since then he had consistently obeyed the divine will and had never once betrayed his conscience. He had seen a great vision and had been consistently loyal to it. But the result had been disaster upon disaster. First, he lost the security of his job; then his family turned against him; next, the leaders of the Jewish society persecuted him and, eventually, the common people rose in opposition. Now he hangs on the Cross, stripped of everything, condemned as a criminal, deserted by his friends—in the eyes of the world a complete and hopeless failure. "My God, my God, why forsake me?"

Sometimes this heart-breaking cry of desolation is explained as the consequence of a mystical bearing of the world's sin by Jesus. If I understand rightly, that means that for some minutes he identified himself so completely with the evil which he had come to destroy that he was wholly separated from the Father. I believe the true explanation is simpler. His world had crashed in ruins around him and he was shattered by the forces of doubt and self-distrust. He had been so confident that he was right. Now the confidence had gone. Worse still, neither human voice nor divine prompting was present to lift the gloom and alleviate the anguish.

I suppose this sense of being forsaken by God comes, at one time or another, to many who try to be true to the divine will. If only we had taken the easier path and gone with the crowd, these troubles would not have overtaken us. Instead we followed the light of our consciences, often sacrificing the things which are highly prized by the world. And now we seem to have achieved nothing but ridicule and contempt. Yes, it is the privilege of those who would give their lives in the service of their fellows to suffer like this. Our history books are full of the deeds of great men who, during their life-times lived in the shadows, despised and rejected, but, like the Christ, came into their own after their deaths.

If, then, you feel certain that God has called you to undertake some work for him, your loyalty must be inflexible. It matters not if you are despised, if your friends desert you, if, at times, it seems that God meets your prayers with silence, you must persevere in following the light as you see it. When you come to die, there is only one question you need to ask, "Have I done my duty to the best of my ability and according to conscience?" If the answer is yes, you will not have to worry about being laid to rest in a pauper's grave with no mourners to do you homage. Better that than an expensive funeral in a great cathedral after a life in which you have betrayed your ideals and silenced your conscience.

It is here that the Church has something to learn, because there is a danger that we shall miss our opportunity to lead the nation by putting expediency before conscience. Too often we allow the question, "Is it wise?" to obscure the more fundamental "Is it right?" For instance, while I have no intention of re-opening the pacifist argument, I always deplored the reason which was put forward by some anti-pacifists for supporting the war—what would happen to the Church if Hitler were to win? The answer to that question is not our business; we must leave it to God. While there may be strong arguments for Christians taking up arms against Fascists, the suggestion that we should do something wrong for fear that God is incapable of looking after himself is unworthy, to say the least. If we want to join the forces, let us do it from the conviction that it is our bounden duty and that God approves our action. If, on the other hand, we think it wrong, we must keep out and leave it to God to take care of the consequences.

Of course, wisdom and tact are valuable gifts, but we need to distinguish between these and timidity and time-serving. In the early days of my ministry I joined with three or four fellow parsons in sending a letter to the local press on a contemporary topic— I believe it was the moral implications of the Munich agreement. Shortly after it appeared a kindly diocesan official phoned me, "That was a most unwise letter you signed," he said. "What you wrote is probably true, but it won't help the Church and it certainly won't help you." The official was a hard-working and devoted priest who was genuinely interested in my welfare, but it did not seem to occur to him that it was the duty of a Christian to obey his conscience and to trust in God, no matter what the consequences might be. Such an attitude is particularly unfortunate when it is directed towards young clergymen who are naturally inclined to play for safety for reasons of security. It is the function of the Church to lead, and not to endorse public opinion. It will inevitably make many enemies. This is better than being dismissed as futile and irrelevant. I am not suggesting that we should look for martyrdom, rather that we must be true to the vision which we have seen, even though other men, better than ourselves, believe the vision to be mistaken.

Secondly, this fourth word from the Cross has a message for those who have loosened their grip on life. I expect some will read these lines who, because of recent suffering or bereavement, have temporarily lost their balance and find themselves groping in the shadows. They are trying to hold on, but it is not easy and sometimes it seems that a big part of them has become numbed. If you feel like that, take courage from the fact that the God to whom you pray has had a similar experience, and worse. It was not only on the Cross that there was agony in the heart of Christ. On Maundy Thursday evening, in the garden of Gethsemane, his friends slept while he drank alone the cup of suffering and his sweat, like drops of blood, fell to the ground. The cup was not removed, but the angels strengthened him. That, too, can be your experience. Remember the important thing about suffering is not that we should be spared it, but that we should be given the courage to face it squarely and to master it. A life which has never experienced loneliness, misrepresentation and anguish is a poor and immature product. How much better to experience them and to rise above them. But beware of self-pity. I am sometimes distressed by the tales of woe I hear when visiting my parishioners. "Of course, vicar, the war hit us all, but nobody knew what I went through. It's all right for Mrs. Smith next door, but she isn't a widow and she will never understand what it meant to have had both sons called up. And now I've been in bed with a heart for three months and I get such headaches at night, I never sleep a wink." All that may be true, but how much better not to talk about it.

I am glad that during the years of unemployment I worked in a distressed area where conditions worse than appalling prevailed. To-day when I begin to feel sorry for myself, I think of those bug-infested hovels where half-starving men and women fought the grim battle of existence. Not only am I reproached by their suffering, but even more by the wonderful and heroic spirit which, in spite of the tears and the heart-break, never lacked in humour and generosity.

So I would suggest that the best cure for the man who has been hit by some big sorrow is to direct his glance towards those who are even less fortunate than himself and let him find peace and re-creation in being of service to them.

If, however, your suffering is really exceptional and your spirit is bruised to such an extent that the light in your life has gone out, and that does happen sometimes, then look at the Cross, even if it is surrounded by shadows, and hear this fourth word of the Saviour who feels that God has forsaken him; and then put your hand in his and let deep call to deep.

> Lead kindly light, amid the encircling gloom,
>   lead thou me on;
> The night is dark and I am far from home, lead
>   thou me on.
> Keep thou my feet; I do not ask to see
> The distant scene—one step enough for me.

If that is your prayer, then Christ will, in his love and pity, look upon you.

In conclusion, a word to those who have been trying to live the Christian life for some years but feel they make little progress. You look back to your Confirmation day or to some great spiritual experience when everything seemed so easy and you were aware of the nearness of God's presence. To-day that has all gone. Your prayers are an effort and your communions an unrefreshing obligation. You are no longer on the hill-top but in a dark valley, and you rarely, if ever, feel the reality of God's spirit. Do not worry about it; we all go through these periods; they are necessary for our spiritual development. I expect the cry on the Cross was the most intense experience of desolation in Christ's life, but there must have been other occasions when he felt that the Father had forgotten him. "Keep on keeping on" is a motto as austere as it is true. But never let us forget the purpose of our quest. We need to be careful when we talk about the crosses which have been laid on us, as quite often they are little more than slight inconveniences, but of this we can be certain—in baptism we are called by Christ to share in his life so that we may further his Kingdom. We shall do this only if we are prepared to face the sufferings and the disappointments which necessarily come to the man who regards inflexible loyalty to the will of God as his most precious possession. At times the heavens will seem silent and we shall be tempted to doubt, but we shall carry on because in our bones we shall know that, beyond the darkness, there is light.

We commend to thy fatherly goodness all those who are in any way afflicted or distressed, in mind, body or estate; that it may please thee to comfort and relieve them, according to their several necessities, giving them patience under their sufferings, and a happy issue out of all their afflictions. And this we beg for Jesus Christ's sake. Amen.

O Lord, we beseech thee mercifully to receive the prayers of thy people which call upon thee; and grant that they may both perceive and know what things they ought to do, and also may have grace and power faithfully to fulfil the same; through Jesus Christ our Lord. Amen.

Lighten our darkness, we beseech thee, O Lord; and by thy great mercy defend us from all perils and dangers of this night; for the love of thy only Son, our Saviour, Jesus Christ. Amen.

VI

After that, as Jesus knew that everything was now finished and fulfilled, he said (to fulfil the scripture), "I am thirsty." (St. John xix, 28.)

IT is a startling paradox that he who had once said, "Anyone who drinks the water I shall give him will never thirst any more; the water I shall give him will turn into a spring of water welling up to eternal life", was now crying out, "I am thirsty".

Reticence forbids any public contemplation of the physical agonies which Jesus must have suffered on Calvary, but human experience can well appreciate the appeal for water which comes from the parched lips of a body that is wracked by pain, and dying.

It is so natural; yet commentators have been inclined to explain away this fifth word from the Cross, interpreting it as a spiritual thirst for the souls of men. I do not doubt that the spiritual thirst was there, for it was part and parcel of his being; but in this particular instance it cannot be made to fit the context. What Jesus wanted was water.

And here, for those who will listen, there is a challenge. "Then the king will say to those on the left, 'Begone from me, you accursed ones, to the

E

eternal fire which has been prepared for the devil and his angels! For I was thirsty but you never gave me drink.' Then they will answer, 'Lord, when did we ever see you thirsty and did not minister unto you?' Then he will answer them, 'I tell you truly, in so far as you did not do it to one of these, even the least of them, you did not do it to me.' So they shall depart to eternal punishment."

It was on Maundy Thursday evening that Jesus tried to drive home the lesson of service. As he washed the disciples' feet, he hoped they would realise that the one prize worth coveting is the opportunity to minister to the needs of others.

We hear this proclaimed so frequently from the pulpit that we have become immune to the sting of its challenge. So, let me ask a straight question. "To what extent do you believe in helping your neighbour?" And, what is more important, "To what extent are you prepared to act upon your belief?" It is not easy to give honest answers, because most of us know that once the veneer of good manners has been stripped from us, our hearts reveal themselves as selfish and grasping. "If you want to make the most of life, look after Number One" is the philosophy of most of us; but it is diametrically opposed to the teaching of Jesus. So let us apply Christ's standard of service in three ways—to our behaviour as private individuals, as members of a community and as democratic citizens.

I accept with reserve the criticisms of the Church which are put forward by its opponents, but we have to admit that one of the most frequent is the assertion that Churchmen do not exert themselves on behalf of their less-fortunate neighbours. In fact, I think from the evidence which came my way during the war, that the Church played an honourable part in welfare and charitable organisations; but that is not the point. Good works should characterise not some, but all Christians; and, while it may be true that a keen nucleus of socially-minded Christians has saved the good name of the Church, we must not rest content until all who profess to follow Christ are eager to imitate him in the service of their fellows. There must be no shirking of our responsibilities in this respect.

At the height of the Bristol blitz I went to a village in north Devon to see about the evacuation of some children from my parish. I called on the billeting officer and suggested that, with his permission, I should make enquiries. He agreed, but added, "Don't go to the vicarage or to the big houses, as they all have dozens of excuses. If you want your kiddies to have a friendly welcome, go to the cottages near the meadow." I did not follow his advice. I went to the vicarage. It was a large building with at least ten bedrooms. The clergyman received me with charm, but declined to help on the ground that his son was likely to spend part of his leave in Devonshire. I persisted, and was sharply informed that I was unaware of the difficulties which beset country parsons and their wives. Maybe I was, but what were they when compared with the difficulties which beset boys and girls in a shelter as the aeroplanes rained death from the sky. "Lord, when saw we thee a stranger and took thee not in?" "I tell you in so far as you did not do it to one of these, even the least of them, you did not do it to me."

Again, one of the big difficulties which face parsons like myself, who work in the east ends of large cities, is the lack of suitable leaders. We are constantly wanting men and women to help us with drama, music, evening classes, community centres and clubs. So we go to the more prosperous churches in the west ends to appeal for volunteers to give us a hand once a week. At once the excuses begin. A man can play tennis or golf three nights a week and go to his club another two, but he cannot find the time to be of service to others.

So face this challenge as it affects your private life. Every day you can hear, if you will listen, the cry, "I thirst".

Next, what of our behaviour as members of the community? To what extent do other people matter to us? My first point was that we should always look for opportunities to give water to the thirsty; my second is different. We must remember that some people are thirsty because injustice prevents them from gaining access to the water supply. Our task is to quench their thirst by overcoming the injustice. Here are two illustrations. I was having tea with a family which is distinguished in Church circles. We discussed housing conditions. I said that I had some small dreary houses in my parish—some of them so overcrowded that five people slept in a room. Sitting opposite me was a girl who, having recently married, was about to move into a house of her own. "They don't deserve anything better," she said. "They only put coals in the bath if you give them a bathroom." I challenged her to supply me with a list of people known to her who kept coals in the bath and suggested that I would go with her to investigate. She apologised and admitted her stupidity. Yes, but what is worrying is that it is possible for a girl to be brought up in a Church family, to say her prayers, to receive the Sacrament weekly, and yet to be dangerously anti-social and reactionary in her outlook. She was ignorant of the conditions in which thousands of her countrymen had to live. She felt no obligation towards them beyond making ill-considered criticisms. While she shared in the Sacrament of Christ's death at the communion table, she made no attempt to share in, still less to relieve, the agonies of the Christ as he suffered in the bodies of the common people.

Take another example. Whatever our views may be about the reports which reach us concerning conditions in Europe, it has to be admitted that some countries are worse off than Britain. To what extent are we prepared to submit ourselves to an extended programme of austerity on their behalf? A Christian cannot evade his responsibilities by laying the blame on Hitler. The fact is that people are hungry and ill-housed, and it is our duty to help. This is simple justice, not altruism. We have to see that the elementary needs of our neighbour are met, no matter who our neighbour may be. We cannot evade our responsibility because we dislike him or because in the past he has done us an injury. Moreover, as Christians, it should not be difficult for us to see the connection between a Jewish labourer crying for water from his cross and a European peasant mother so famished and weak that she has not the strength to suckle the baby lying thirsty at her breast.

Thirdly, there is our behaviour as democratic citizens. A Christian must be a realist and, whether the world likes it or not, he must attack those deep-rooted social evils which cause suffering. Let us suppose that in a village there is only one well and it is the property of the squire. Some villagers are unemployed and cannot afford to buy water so, as Christians in fairly comfortable circumstances, we go to the squire and buy cups of water for them. That is a necessary work of mercy to relieve an immediate need, but we must go further. We need to state publicly that it is wrong for one man to have the monopoly of the water supply and that we shall not be content until each man has his own tap in his own home. The fact that the squire may call us political intriguers and red revolutionaries need not worry us a scrap, because it is our duty as Christians not merely to dress wounds but to remove, by a drastic surgical operation, the cancer which causes the wound. And we must stick to our guns even though he threatens to resign the churchwardenship and to cancel his subscriptions to parochial funds.

We must be equally firm when the cause of distress is to be found in another direction. If the community suffers because men are lazy or seek sectional gain through unofficial strikes, we must make our stand against them even though we are regarded by them as the tools of political reactionaries.

It is here that the Church has been weak and timid in recent generations. Little more than a hundred years ago many Churchmen were ready to provide bibles for the negro slaves, but only a very few had the courage to go to the slave owners and to denounce, in the name of the Lord, the iniquitous practice of slavery. Similarly, between the two wars, Christians helped to run clubs for the unemployed, but, too often, they lacked the courage and integrity to point to the hideous injustices in our social system which made for unemployment. I state this as a fact that when I preached sermons in wealthy churches for my distressed parish, money was generously given providing I said nothing to question a system which allowed one section of the community to exploit the other, but the moment I proclaimed those social and economic truths which now, as the result of the war, nearly everybody accepts, the subscriptions almost dried up.

Even to-day Churchmen are not conspicuous for their leadership in social matters. They are prepared to state principles which inconvenience nobody, but they stop short of their application for fear that they will annoy somebody. Too often they try to explain away their ineffectiveness by saying that the Church must not get mixed up with politics. But this argument does not bear investigation because principles can only be applied to social life by political action. I am not suggesting for a moment that the Church should identify itself with a particular political party, but I do assert that individual Churchmen should bear responsible witness to their beliefs by making their presence felt in the places where practical decisions are made. No doubt they will become unpopular in some circles as a consequence; but when that happens, there will be hope!

What is your attitude towards social, political and economic problems? Is it based upon self-interest, or upon the determination to create an ordering of society based upon justice, brotherhood and fair dealing? Can you say that the conditions of the district in which you live are improving because of the intelligent interest and action which you and your fellow Churchmen are taking? When a municipal or a national election takes place, does the knowledge that you are a Christian determine the way in which you vote?

As we hear this fifth word from the Cross, let it challenge us to listen to the cries of suffering humanity to-day, remembering that, whenever we can give a cup of cold water to the thirsty, we are ministering to the needs of Christ. For we can be certain that whenever we can minimise poverty, squalor, stupidity and want we shall be forwarding his purpose of love.

Father, give us grace not to pass by suffering or joy

without eyes to see; give us understanding and wise sympathy; preserve us from clumsiness, that we may be sorry with those who weep and glad with those who rejoice; use us, as thou canst, to make happy and strong the hearts of others and humbly to set forth thy light which is the light of the world. Amen.

Blessed Lord, who wast content for our sakes to bear sorrow and want and death: grant to us such a measure of thy spirit that we may follow thee in all self-denial and tenderness of soul. Help us, by thy great love, to succour the afflicted, to relieve the needy and destitute, to comfort the feeble-minded, to share the burdens of the heavy laden, and ever to see thee in all that are poor or desolate. Amen.

O God, our King, teach us to bear one another's burdens and the burdens of the commonwealth. Open our eyes to see the woes of our land, the despair of the lives of many of our fellow citizens, the deep and shameful wrongs that cry out to be put right. Give to us also a vision of our land as thou wouldst have it be and as thou alone can remake it. Take us, we humbly beseech thee, to be thy servants, giving us no rest or discharge until thou hast wrought this work of pity, that the generations yet unborn may praise thy name. Amen.

VII

And when Jesus took the vinegar, he said, "It is finished", bowed his head, and gave up his spirit. (St. John xix, 30.)

"No one is any use to the Reign of God who puts his hand to the plough and then looks behind him." We usually call people who plough a straight and consistent line fanatics. We say they have single-track minds and we regret they cannot learn to be a little more reasonable and moderate. It is certain that, as the last moments passed on Good Friday afternoon, many sightseers pointed to the dying Jesus and remarked, "What a pity the young man was such a fanatic! If only he had been a little wiser, it need never have come to this." From their point of view the criticism was justified. Jesus had set out to plough a particular line and never once did he take his eyes from it. Now, having reached his goal, he can look back and say, "It is finished". Yes, but at what a cost!

In one sense a Christian must always be a fanatic. He has a job to do, and nothing must interfere with it. St. Paul said, "The last drops of my own sacrifice are falling; my time to go has come. I have fought in the good fight; I have run my course; I have kept the faith. Now the crown of a good life awaits me, with which the Lord, that just Judge, will reward me on the great Day—and not only me but all who have loved and longed for his appearance." Like his master, he had, with grit and determination, applied himself to his task, and he had not swerved.

An epitaph which has always impressed me is that which appears on the tombstone of a Cavalier soldier who, having sold most of his possessions for the Royalist cause, met his death on the battlefield against the Roundheads. "He served King Charles with a constant, dangerous, and an expensive loyalty."

To what extent have we got our eyes on our goal, ploughing a straight furrow? When the time comes for us to leave this world shall we be able to say, "It is finished"? Will it be possible for us to remark with St. Paul, "I have fought in the good fight; I have run my course; I have kept the faith"? The answers depend upon whether or not we have served King Jesus with a constant, dangerous and an expensive loyalty.

In recent times we have heard much about the need for a religious revival and for a drastic overhaul of the Church. I agree. The times are desperate and the Church will have to make revolutionary changes if it is to rise to the occasion. Yes, but while we must be prepared to throw overboard worthless traditions and to employ new methods, we must never forget that ultimately the success or failure of the Church depends upon the spiritual toughness and integrity of its members. A revised Prayer Book may help to make our services more intelligible, but it can never be a substitute for those spiritual qualities which should characterise the life of a Christian. As any parish priest knows only too well, a common-sense, business-like approach in the conduct of worship and in the management of parochial affairs helps to commend the Church to the people in the locality, but it will achieve little unless it is supported by an example of sincerity and devotion on the part of himself and his congregation. The early Church was successful because at the centre there were sufficient people with a white-hot passion for the things in which they believed; who were prepared to take risks and to make sacrifices; who did not mind being called religious fanatics. But do not imagine they behaved in this way because they were born with unusual advantages; on the contrary it was because they were prepared for their rough, human, sinful nature to be disciplined in the hard school of Christian experience. And it is just that truth which I want to get across to you as we listen to this sixth word from the Cross.

In Lent and Holy Week God sometimes lets us renew our vision. The appeal of the Cross stirs us and we see more clearly the part we should be playing to further the Kingdom. But we must be realists and face the facts. If this experience is to be more than a fleeting emotion, it means a stern discipline and a faithful discipleship. At the time of Dunkirk the people of these islands showed a magnificent spirit, but it was not long before they realised that this spirit had to be directed into the performance of arduous and dreary routine duties—hours and hours of fire-watching, Home Guard and A.R.P. It is just the same with religion. I hope your imagination is fired with a longing to serve your crucified master and to play your part in the religious revival of the country, but, if you are to rise to the occasion, it means an exacting discipline.

Let me give two illustrations, the discipline of Church membership and the discipline of prayer.

If you wish to win England to Christ, you must accept the fact that the instrument God has created for the purpose is the Church. You may criticise the Church, you may feel that it is comparatively useless, but the truth remains that apart from the Church there is no society capable of doing the task; so if the Church fails, your vision will not be accomplished. What, then, is the quality of your Church member-

ship? When you were baptised Christ signed you on
as one of his workmen. What sort of a workman are
you? Is your work good and solid? What part are
you playing in the life of your parish? Do you help
to make things hum? I must confess that I am often
baffled by the conceptions of good Churchmanship
which prevail in some quarters. We are given to
understand that a man is a 'good churchman' because
he holds certain views on fasting communion, litur-
gical order or ceremonial observances. Nothing could
be further from the spirit and teaching of Jesus. A
man is a good churchman if his life is guided by the
knowledge that he belongs to a society which God
has created to further his Kingdom. Unless this
loyalty dominates his other loyalties, then no amount
of ecclesiastical correctness will be of any avail. A
parish is strong in churchmanship if it is making a
Christian impact upon the general life of the neigh-
bourhood. If it is not doing that, its services, regulations and ceremonies tend to futility. It may be
desirable that Churchmen should go to communion
every Sunday—I personally think that it is—but the
test of churchmanship is not the attendance at the
service, but what happens when the service is over.
Are the communicants building up a virile community
in the locality? Are they seeing to it that justice,
culture, and freedom, are increasing in their parish

as a result of their labours? If we want to assess the situation correctly, we should ask this question, "If the church which I attend were to close down, would there be a marked deterioration in the general life of the vicinity?" We must realise that attendance at services is not identical with good churchmanship. Good churchmanship demands the continual effort on our part to make the Christian community the strongest influence in the place where we live.

I know it is not always easy to practise this when we are living in an uncongenial parish, where the authorities are slack, or the services are gabbled through in an inaudible voice, or customs not compatible with the Prayer Book are forced upon us. And I frankly admit that I have at times found myself in churches where the conditions have been so intolerable that I could not conscientiously attend regularly or help with the work. But, in normal circumstances, it is our duty to sink our likes and dislikes and to implement the promises which were made at our baptisms. Most of us clergy are overworked hacks who, in spite of our many limitations, sins and deficiences, are trying to do our best. Your job is to come alongside us and help. If you will do that, perhaps your enthusiasm will make good our omissions.

Secondly, the discipline of prayer. Men become

spiritually tough when they learn to live in the presence of God; and that necessitates regular prayer. We hear much of atomic energy, but there is a divine energy capable of greater things, and it is this energy which lays hold of us and saturates us in prayer. Nothing can take its place. Just as Jesus spent long hours on his knees in silent communion with his Father, so must we strive to draw near to him and be filled with the same Spirit. Are you a praying person? Do you throw open the windows of your soul to let in the mighty influence of God's divine energy, which gives a purpose to your life, the power to remain steadfast, the courage to surmount difficulties?

I have never been a member of the Oxford Group, and about some of its methods I am sceptical, but I do admire the discipline which their members observe with regard to prayer. Some years ago a priest, well over seventy, stayed with me at Christmas. As he had assisted at the Midnight Mass I arranged for him to take the late celebration on the following morning, thinking that it would give him a few hours' extra sleep. When I got up for the eight o'clock service, I was surprised to find that he had already been at his prayers for an hour. He was a Grouper and nothing was allowed to interfere with the 'morning watch' of prayer and Bible study.

On another occasion I preached in a church which had a Group connection; during the sermon five or six members of the congregation remained in the vestry to pray for me and my hearers. I came to the conclusion that sermons might be less ineffective if preachers could always count on such support.

If you feel that your spiritual life is weak, take yourself to task over your prayers. Begin each morning at your bedside with God and think through the coming day with him. Mention your engagements and the people you are to meet, face your problems and worries, and ask the Holy Spirit to guide you. Then when night comes look back over the past hours, offer thanks for the little things which have brought happiness, be honest about your failures, hold up those who are in need, and finish by spending a few minutes in quiet restfulness. If you do this regularly you will find that, as the years go by, you will become increasingly conscious of God's abiding presence and you will start to look at life through his eyes. Do not evade the issue by pretending that such a discipline is intended only for those who have an aptitude for prayer, for it is as necessary for your soul as the discipline of regular meals is for your body. Moreover the men who get things done and translate their visions into realities are those who have their feet set on the earth, but their eyes directed towards the heavens.

"It is finished." Jesus will shortly breathe his last. The clouds are lifting, the sense of defeat is passing and he is certain that, in spite of the apparent failure, his task is done.

One day our hour will come. That is not a morbid thought, but a straightforward challenge. Whether the end is near or distant, only one thing matters— that we set out towards our goal with inflexible determination, refusing to be turned back by hardships, disappointments, unpopularity or temptations. If we persist faithfully, it will be said of us, as it was said of Charles's Cavalier, that we served our King with a constant, dangerous, and an expensive loyalty.

O God, who hast prepared for them that love Thee such good things as pass man's understanding; Pour into our hearts such love toward thee, that we, loving thee above all things, may obtain thy promises, which exceed all that we can desire; through Jesus Christ our Lord. Amen.

O Christ, the Master Carpenter, who at the last through wood and nails, purchased man's whole salvation, wield well thy tools in the workshop of the world, so that we, who come rough-hewn to thy bench, may be fashioned to a truer beauty by thine hand. Amen.

O Thou, who art the light of the world, the desire of all nations, and the shepherd of our souls, let thy light shine in the darkness, and by the lifting up of thy Cross gather the peoples unto thee, that all the ends of the earth may see the salvation of God. Amen.

VIII

And when Jesus had cried with a loud voice, he said, "Father, into thy hands I commend my spirit", and with these words he expired. When the army captain saw what had happened he glorified God, saying, "This man was really innocent." And when all the crowds who had collected for the sight saw what had happened, they turned away beating their breasts. (St. Luke xxiii, 46-48.)

So the curtain drops on the final scene of Calvary's tragedy. The agony is at an end; the clouds lift. Jesus, commending his soul to the Father, bows his head, and it is all over. Somehow it seems incredible. I remember as a boy going to the Three Hours' Service and hoping against hope that something would happen before three o'clock to save the situation. The same feeling came over me when, years later, I witnessed the passion play at Oberammergau. The story was reaching its climax; the soldiers were about to nail Jesus to the Cross. Surely somebody would intervene before the circumstances became too desperate? I know it is absurd, but have you felt like that about it? Somehow or other one's whole being revolts at the thought of Christ's crucifixion. We think of him at Bethlehem surrounded by the Christmas angels; in the carpenter's shop helping at the bench, walking among the lanes and hills of Galilee healing the sick and teaching the poor, riding in triumph in the Palm Sunday procession while the people hailed him as their king—always bringing hope and health, colour and gaiety. We think of all this and cannot believe that God will permit injustice and tyranny to ruin a life so magnificent. But He does. Nothing can save him now. A last breath, a final sigh, and the heart of Jesus ceases to beat.

> Long years ago, as earth lay dark and still,
> Rose a loud cry upon a lonely hill,
> While in the frailty of our human clay,
> Christ, our redeemer, passed the self-same way.

Such is the tragedy of Calvary. If only men had behaved differently it would never have come to this. But it has; and now if our hearts can feel shame we shall want to be alone with our wretchedness, in the hope that we shall be led to realise how deeply we are implicated in the appalling failure which resulted in the rejection of the Son of God.

But so far as Christ himself was concerned, it was not tragedy but victory. He had won through, and, as the moment came for his soul to leave his body, he expressed, in this final word from the Cross, his complete trust in his Father. People might jeer at him, soldiers flog him, disciples desert him and friends betray him, but nothing could destroy the personal relationship between himself and God. It is to this fact I would draw your attention as we take our last look at the Cross and watch the life of Christ drawing to its close.

Ultimately the one question which has to be faced, because upon it depends our destiny, is this—What is the quality of the relationship between ourselves and the living God? There are, of course, many other considerations for Christians—loyalty to the Church, participation in the Sacraments, enthusiasm for social righteousness—but more important than any of them, because it is fundamental, is our relationship with Christ.

Let me put this as simply as I can. To be a Christian means to accept Christ into one's life as Saviour and Lord. In the dream which is the theme of the last book in the Bible, Jesus says, "Lo, I stand at the door and knock; if anyone hears my voice and opens the door, I will come in and sup with him, and he with me." If, therefore, you want a religion which works, if you are eager to discover the secret of Christianity, throw open the door of your heart to Christ and ask him to come in and take control.

Now, have you done that? It is no good saying that you go to church, have been confirmed and attend Communion. All those things are important and must not be ignored, but they are valueless unless they are based upon a personal relationship with the living Christ.

It is refreshing that the term 'conversion' is finding its way back into the parlance of the Church of England, because I am sure that in recent years we have allowed matters of secondary importance to obscure the straightforward evangelistic challenge. When I was a freshman at Cambridge I attended two religious meetings during my first week. At the first we discussed Truth, Beauty and Goodness; at the second the speaker took me into a corner and asked me if I was saved. Although I deplored the atmosphere of the latter meeting and the methods which were employed, I am sure that the organisers got nearer to the fundamentals than those who sponsored the first. It is useful to argue about the eternal verities, but such argument rarely touches man's basic spiritual need. Unfortunately our reasonable dislike for the emotional setting in which the gospel of conversion has been proclaimed has caused us to ignore its truth. It is probably wrong to challenge men indiscriminately with the issue of personal redemption; better to wait until the ground has been prepared and the right moment comes—but, sooner or later, the challenge must come.

The trouble with some evangelists is that they expect their hearers to undergo a particular experience of conversion. They forget that in the New Testament Christ deals with men one by one with methods suitable for each. Paul's life was altered by a dramatic moment on the Damascus road; John responded to the friendship of Jesus as a flower does to the sun; Peter experienced several crises, each of which seemed of unique importance at the time, but in retrospect proved to be steps along the path to full discipleship; Timothy, who never knew Christ in the flesh, was brought up in a home which was steeped in a Christian atmosphere. All four were quite different, but each eventually reached the stage when he could speak of his Lord as him "Whose I am and whom I serve".

Hence what matters for us is the fact of conversion and not the method. Although we may be nauseated by the prospect of standing up at a meeting and saying that we are saved, yet we need to be quite certain in our hearts that Christ has placed his grip upon us and that we know him as a living person. In the last resort the reality of our religion is determined by the extent to which we are conscious of the abiding presence of Jesus.

When we have finished our study of the Cross, what matters is that we shall have Christ with us in our hearts. We have been made for God and we shall never find satisfaction until our spirits are knit with His. We may try to evade the issue by taking an overdose of ecclesiasticism, by attending too many services, by busying ourselves unduly in good works, but in the end we shall have to face the personal challenge of a God who created us for fellowship with himself.

The danger is that we shall be moved by the poignancy of the crucifixion, yet come to no decision and allow the opportunity to slip. We shall look at the Cross and say, "Ah, what a pity!" But we shall not allow the crucified to take possession of our hearts.

Some years ago I spent Good Friday alone in the mountains in north Wales. It was a beautiful day and, at three o'clock, I remember looking round at the countryside. It was perfect—the green of the new leaves, the colour and smell of the spring flowers, the sheep on the hillside, and, in the distance, the wide expanse of sea glistening in the sun. And the thought struck me, "It must have looked much like this on the first Good Friday—leaves, flowers, animals, water—and it will continue to look the same in a thousand years. Christ's death makes no difference one way or the other. The world of nature just goes on and on, oblivious of the tremendous conflicts in the souls of men." Some minutes later I turned a corner and could see below me the beach of Llandudno with the holiday crowds swarming like ants; I wondered if to them, too, the death of Christ meant nothing. On the first Good Friday men had taken no notice. If they knew about the crucifixion they had dismissed it as the execution of one more criminal. As the centuries have passed the Cross of Christ has been held up Holy Week after Holy Week and, alas, most men have been as indifferent as the sheep which nibble on the mountain side. They have ignored the greatest fact in history which has a direct bearing upon the fate of each individual soul. But not all. Some have noticed. They have perceived the challenge and have responded. They have looked at the face of the Crucified, have heard his call, and have offered to him their lives.

The main purpose of this book is to bring you to face this challenge squarely. Are you prepared to offer your life to Christ? Will you humbly admit that your urgent need is for a Saviour to free you from sin and to give you newness of life? Are you ready to claim the promise of the Holy Spirit and, under his influence, to follow where he leads?

I am not suggesting that to answer these questions

77

in the affirmative will solve all your problems. On the contrary it will only mark your entry into a new realm of existence and activity. You will need a life-time of discipline and growth, striving day by day to become more like Christ, allowing his influence to saturate every department of your being.

On Easter Sunday you will hear at the Communion table the words, "This is my body which is given for you. This is my blood which is shed for you." Will you try to say in reply, "And this, Lord, is my body which I give to you. And this, Lord, is my blood which, if need be, is ready to be shed for you"? That question is not a platitude. I mean you to take each word seriously. If you receive the Sacrament with a proper understanding it is as though Christ were to lift you on to his Cross and to link you with his passion and crucifixion. When that happens, the disruptive energies of the Holy Spirit will pour through your soul and God will use your life to further his redeeming work in the world.

John Wesley said, "Give me one hundred men who fear no one but God, hate nothing but Sin, and have the love of Jesus in their hearts; and with them I can move the world." Will you be one of that hundred? Will you come to the Cross and allow the Christ, now risen, and victorious, to place his grip

78

upon you and to energise your life with his mighty power, so that in company with him you may go out to dare all in the service of his Kingdom? If you are prepared for such a sacrifice, you will embark upon a life which, in spite of all the difficulties, failures and hardships, will enable you to say at its destination, "Father, into thy hands I commend my spirit".

"Do you think Jesus is dead?" asked Pilate's wife in a legend, as she stood by the Cross on Good Friday afternoon.

"No, lady, I don't," replied the centurion, who had watched him hanging there on Calvary.

"Then, where is he?"

"Let loose in all the world, lady, where neither Roman nor Jew nor any other man can stop the victory of His Risen Life."

By thine Agony and bloody Sweat; by thy Cross and Passion; by thy precious Death and Burial; by thy glorious Resurrection and Ascension; and by the coming of the Holy Ghost,

Good Lord, deliver us. Amen.

> I sometimes think about the Cross,
> And shut my eyes and try to see
> The cruel nails and crown of thorns,
> And Jesus crucified for me.

79

But even could I see him die,
I could but see a little part
Of that great love which like a fire
Is always burning in His heart. Amen.

Lord Jesus, our Leader, we give ourselves to Thee for
the cause of thy glorious Kingdom; for joy or for sorrow,
for success or for failure, for life or for death, now and
for evermore. Amen.